Down Our Street
By Brian McCann

Cover Photograph: Back Chester Street, Birkenhead 1901

Published 2009 by Appin Press, an imprint of Countyvise Ltd.,
14 Appin Road, Birkenhead, Wirral CH41 9HH.

Copyright © 2003, 2009 Brian McCann

The right of Brian McCann to be identified as the author of this
work has been asserted by him in accordance with the Copyright,
Design and Patents Act 1988.

British Library Cataloguing in Publication Data.
A catalogue record for this book is available from the British
Library.

ISBN 978 1 906205 24 9

All rights reserved. No part of this publication may be reproduced,
stored in a retrieval system, or transmitted, in any other form, or by
any other means, electronic, chemical, mechanical, photocopying,
recording or otherwise, without the prior permission of the
publisher, author or The Active Drama Company (UK) LTD, The
Grand Entrance, Birkenhead Park, Park Road North, Birkenhead,
CH41 4HD, 0151 652 0100.

Music and original CD can be obtained from The Active Drama
Company (UK) LTD, The Grand Entrance, Birkenhead Park, Park
Road North, Birkenhead. CH 41 4HD

Forward

Down Our Street was written whilst working with students from Wirral Metropolitan College in 2002. The initial idea was to create a piece of theatre for the community…a play that would attract a wider audience because of the subject matter rather than the theatre.

The world famous shipbuilders Cammell Laird was the perfect choice.

For well over a century 'the yard' was the employer of thousands upon thousands of workers from Birkenhead, the Wirral, Liverpool and from far and wide. Birkenhead was built around the Shipbuilding industry and most families, if not all had some connection to Cammell Laird.

The initial idea of the play was to celebrate this through the eyes of the people and I hope this is what *Down Our Street* does.

As you read through the play the scenes shift very fast from one to another interjected with statements, poetry and of course song. This takes the audience on a fast moving journey over the one hundred and fifty years the play covers, celebrating time, facts, individuals and the spirit that has existed and does still exist today in a proud town.

The characters can be played rather than acted complimenting the fast pace of the dialogue and quick scene changes. They could almost be caricatures played with energy and spirit.

They should celebrate the people and times whilst enjoying the eccentricities of individuals within the script and individual performances. There are many opportunities within the script for performers to share with the audience a reverent yet almost tongue in cheek look at the people and situations although there are times when the reality and seriousness exist and must be played so.

There is plenty of opportunity for slides and film clips to compliment the action and some have been suggested in the script.

The first professional production was in 2003, and, directed by Pauline Daniels, brought in packed houses. The play was fantastically received by both audiences and critics alike in a very warm and vibrant production.

Brian McCann 2008

Dedicated to the memory of our Dad

Harry McCann

He knew half the people in the town...and the other half knew him!

DOWN OUR STREET
By Brian McCann

First performed in 2003 at the Wirral Museum, Birkenhead by the Active Drama Company.
The play ran to full houses for three weeks.

Directed by Pauline Daniels

Cast:

Pauline Daniels
Sylvia Gattril
Micky Finn
Peter Casino
Simon Robinson
Simon Twist
Louise Rhodes
Sally Anne Harman
George Jones
Lucy Brite

Produced by Brian McCann
for The Active Drama Company

Down Our Street, Book, Lyrics and Music ©Brian McCann 2003, 2009

SCENE 1

SFX SHIP YARD, FOG HORNS, HUSTLE AND BUSTLE: THE SETTING IS A STREET. SMALL TERRACED HOUSES ON EITHER SIDE WITH THE SILHOUETTE OF CAMMELL LAIRD'S IN THE BACKGROUND: LIGHTS UP – STREET GETTING SET FOR WORK, HUSBANDS LEAVING: CHILDREN PLAYING, WIVES WAVING AND CHATTERING AS:

WILLIAM LAIRD
I believe Birkenhead is the place to be. I believe Birkenhead should, and will, be the centre of our country's industrial growth, the place where man shall dwell with man what ever their income or status, whatever the situation the Lord has granted them. I believe Birkenhead to be the new town of this country with good housing through efficient and innovative planning, adequate hygiene, a local hospital, public libraries, public parks and facilities for the good people of this town that shall be the envy of the country. People will flock from miles around to see how a town should work and how under the shadow of the greatest ship builder in this country, a town can grow and prosper. I William Laird will see this through and with the opening of the new shipyard at the Birkenhead Pool, Lairds will be nearer for the workers as well as providing more work for the local people and people who choose to come and live in this wonderful place. I believe they shall travel from far a field to work here.

MAN
Three Cheers for Mr Laird!

THE CROWD ARE LED IN CHEERING AND THE MUSIC CONTINUES UNDER SCENE:

WOMAN
They're coming daily.

WOMAN
Who?

WOMAN
Workers! From all over the place! Wales…across the Pennines, and some from abroad.

WOMAN
No!

WOMAN
I'm telling you. They're coming from everywhere - to live here!

WOMAN
Mr. Laird said this would happen.

WOMAN
Mr Laird said a lot would happen!

WOMAN
He said they'd be flocking here by the dozen.

WOMAN
From all over the place!

WOMAN
But where will they live?

WOMAN
They're building more temporary houses till they build the grander ones

WOMAN
I'll believe that when I see it!

WOMAN
I'm quite happy with my two up - two down.

WOMAN
I couldn't be doing with one of those big ones like on Hamilton Square.

WOMAN
They're all going to be like that!

WOMAN
The Clements' girl 'does' for one of those families on the square. She says she's polishing from noon till night, the place is so big.

WOMAN
It takes me all my time to keep my small place clean.

WOMAN
It's surprising you lot all fit in there.

WOMAN
How many have you got now?

WOMAN
Nineteen.

WOMAN
Catholics will be Catholics.

WOMAN
Look.

A FAMILY ENTER WITH SUITCASES LOOKING BEDRAGGLED AND TIRED. THEY STOP CENTRE AND DROP THE CASES:

FRANCESCA
Argyle Street South. This is it!

COORNEELA
This?

A LOOK OF SHOCK DESCENDS ON THE FACES OF THE NEW FAMILY. LIGHTS UP ON WILLIAM LAIRD:

WILLIAM LAIRD
There shall be jobs for everyone. I envisage a work force of over fifty thousand men. We shall build the greatest ships for this great country. We shall build the greatest ships in the world.

BACK TO THE STREET:

PAULI
Very nice, it's really, really nice….cosy…very nice…yes

FRANCESCA
Don't be ridiculous. What's that smell? What's the noise? Why do these houses join so close? Papa, tell me.

CORNEELA
Papa, it's so small, why did we have to come here?

PEOPLE FROM THE OTHER HOUSES START TO ENTER AND STARE:

JARANI
I miss Italy already, Mama!

FRANCESCA
Come, come, this is our home now. Here, Papa can get some work to help us. Now we all can go and eat – here, this one.

CARNEELA
Look at the people stare so mama.

JARANI
They're looking strangely at me.

PAULI
Do as Mama say, go in and we can get something to eat.

WOMAN
Yooooouuueeee!

WOMAN
Bonjour!

WOMAN
Hark at her – we've got a bi-sexual in our midst.

WOMAN
Bilingual.

WOMAN
I was only saying.

WOMAN
Nice to meet you.

WOMAN
I'm Mary Bickerstaff, number four. My door is always open!

WOMAN
Only because your Harold smacked it after a night down the *Happy Valley* and it won't close!

WOMAN
Margaret Chance, number eight – so nice to see you here, I'm sure.

WOMAN
Gladys Poultry, six – I take washing in.

WOMAN
And I iron…ooh…I beg you pardon, Veronica Mews, number nine, at your service.

WOMAN
Good grief!

WOMAN
Always overdoes it!

WOMAN
Always there...up front! Her husband says he woke up one morning and there she was. Married to him, children, house everything. He knew nothing about it!

WOMAN
If there's anything you want....

WOMAN
Anything you need.

WOMAN
Just say.

WOMAN
One of us will have it.

WOMAN
One of us will help you.

WOMAN
Our doors are always open.

THE LADIES ALL ENTER THEIR HOUSES SLAMMING THEIR DOORS SIMULTAINIOUSLY. THE FAMILY ENTER THEIR HOUSE:

<u>SCENE TWO</u>

SLIDE: '*PAXTON*"

PAXTON:
Ladies and Gentlemen, Lord Mayor and Lady, I am pleased to announce this the first day of opening of Birkenhead Park.

APPLAUSE:

Not only have we reclaimed marshy, boggy lands, using a innovative system of drainage….not only have we created a beautiful place to meander and sport, to take refuge from the busy trappings of Victorian life….but we have created the first ever man-made public parkland in the world. Birkenhead being the most fitting place for such a venture as the country's finest example of a new town destined to succeed and grow into one of the greatest towns in this fine country of ours.

APPLAUSE:

FROM THE CROWD COMES THREE MEN DRESSED AS THEY SHOULD BE FROM THEIR OWN TIME: FIRSTLY CHARLES DICKENS:

SLIDE: '*CHARLES DICKENS*'

DICKENS
Liverpool is the most beautiful of cities. I stay here quite a lot for one reason or another. I find the people charming and the area full of interests and oddities. I particularly enjoy travelling across the Mersey to the Wirral where the air is so much cleaner.

LIGHTS UP ON THE FAMILY:

CORNEELA
I don't like it, it's not home. Why can't we go back home?

PAULI
Don't be silly, it's nice here. It'll just take time getting used to. Give it a chance.

FRANCESCA
The people seem really nice.

CORNEELA
Nosey.

JARANI
Interfering.

COREELA
Gossips!

JARANI
Why did we move here when it's cold wet and smells the way it does?

PAULI
This town offers great opportunities. This town is the place to be. We should be thankful that I have a job at all.

MUSIC STARTS
DOWN OUR STREET:

**MUSIC CONTINUES UNDER DIALOGUE.
LIGHTS UP ON WILLIAM SHAKESPEARE:**

SLIDE: '*WILLIAM SHAKESPEARE*'

SHAKESPEARE
Many people have forgotten about the time I spent on the Wirral. A beautiful headland with fertile lands and hard workers to turn the soil. Methinks, perchance, a good place to think, to muse, to talk, to play, and to write. I spent wonderful times here.

LIGHTS UP ON EDWARD 1

SLIDE: EDWARD 1

EDWARD 1
Cold, dank, miserable place, full of monks! However, the food was good and the wild boar was sensational. As for the friar's homebrew! Need I say more! I visited Birkenhead several times for very sombre reasons – sorting one thing or another out and found the whole experience rather amusing. I should not have had to go there at all but where it not the ideal location for all to meet from all around the country – a perfect central point and well guarded on three sides by water.

MUSIC CONTINUES AS SONG STARTS:

SONG 1: DOWN OUR STREET

*Down our street
Where the people that you meet seem really happy
Down our street*

*Down our street
Where the people there will greet you with a smile or two
Down our street*

Our doors are always open
The Kettle's always on
You're welcome for a cuppa
Wherever you are from
Don't hesitate to ask us
To lend a helping hand
We're working hard to make this the best town in the land

Down our street
Where everyone is always glad to see ye'
Down our street

Down our street
You'll hear the sound of chatter and of laughter
Down our street

There's people there to help you
Or to have a good old moan
That's what makes the bricks and mortar
Into a home
And when you need a bob or two
Or a bed just for the night
These people here will help you
These people are alright

Down our street
Where the people that you meet seem really happy
Down our street

Down our street
Where the people there will greet you with a smile or two
Down our street

The cold long nights of winter when the fire's always alight
Doesn't dampen the spirits in the long winter nights
Doesn't fade the feeling that this is where you're from
Everybody knows you for here's where you belong

Down our street
Where the people that you meet seem really happy
Down our street

Down our street
Where the people there will greet you with a smile or two
This is just for you
Down our street

SONG END

SCENE THREE

LIGHTS UP ON 'SHIPYARD':

MAN
You there, watch where you're walking, we don't want any more accidents. If you'd all be so kind as to gather.

MEN COME TOGETHER:

MAN
This announcement is to all men working on the *Enrica*, are you listening – all men working on the *Enrica*... Men! There'll be an extra shilling in your pockets if we get this one finished before schedule.

MAN
And plenty of cockwood for the wives!

MAN
Once it's finished I'm sure they'll be plenty of cockwood to keep the women happy and the families warm – but make the most of it - I can't see us making too many more wooden vessels! Right men, I've said what I have to say, now back to work.

MAN
Aye, Aye captain!

MAN
The royals have spoken!

MEN GO BACK TO WORK:

MAN
Jacko, do you know anything about this one?

MAN
Well it's a fine ship and of some importance.

MAN
Does anyone know anything about it?

MAN
No, it all seem a bit hush, hush.

MAN
There is a rumour it's off West.

MAN
To the Americas.

MAN
You're joking!

MAN
They've been fighting each other for a while now.

MAN
We shouldn't be involved.

MAN
We're best keeping out of the whole situation.

MAN
But that's what they say – this vessel is heading for America.

MAN
I've heard they're even covering up its real name as to stop any connection.

MAN
It's all a bit cloak and dagger for the yard.

MAN
What are the supposed to be calling it?

MAN
The golden eagle?

MAN
Stars and stripes?

MAN
No…The Alabama!

LIGHTS UP ON JOHN LAIRD AS HE SPEAKS WOMEN COME INTO THE STREET AND START HANGING OUT THE WASHING:

JOHN LAIRD
I have no doubt my father will be proud of my election as Birkenhead's first MP in this year of 1863. I shall strive to continue my fathers vision of what a great town this is and, although the housing and planning never went the way he wanted I shall make sure that public health is concentrated on with the opening of the General Hospital this very year. Public concern and interests are still raising issues but with the introduction of our innovative tram system and the new public library to be opened in Hamilton Street I am sure we continue to create a prosperous town as it will continue to be during my political career and beyond. Laird's itself continues to go from strength to strength providing home for many families around the area.

MUSIC: *DOWN OUR STREET:*

Down our street
Where the people that you meet seem really happy
Down our street

Down our street
Where the people there will greet you with a smile or two
Down our street

LIGHTS DOWN

SCENE FOUR

MAN WALKS DOWN THE STREET KNOCKING ON THE WINDOWS. IT IS DAWN:

VOICE OFF
'Ok love…Billy….Billy! It's five to and you've got twenty minutes to get to the yard. If you're late again They're sure to get rid. You know what Jack Lancaster said last time.

LIGHTS UP. A KITCHEN:

BILLY
Alright love.

WIFE
Come on, throw this cuppa down you and get off.

BILLY
I need something to warm me bones – it was a cold night last night.

WIFE
I'm surprised you didn't catch your death, coming in at that unearthly hour.

BILLY
I couldn't miss that meeting.

WIFE
I never said you should've. But I know that meetings don't continue past nine at night and certainly do not transport themselves, lock and stock to the nearest pub.

BILLY
We had a lot to discuss.

WIFE
Aye, I'm sure you did. I heard you discuss all the way up the road to

the tunes of *Lilly Marlene*, *Roll out the Barrel* and *I'm Just a Bird in a Gilded Cage*. Tell me that's a satisfactory conclusion to an important agenda and I'll tell you that it's a load of old baloney!

BILLY
We did get a bit carried away.

WIFE
Carried away, you were practically carried home.

BILLY
Things are happening down the yard that we need to keep and eye on, united like. We need to stand together and understand our rights.

WIFE
Tommy Doyle 'been spouting off again?

BILLY
No, no. He just knows more than everybody else – he keeps his ear to the ground as it where. There's talk of a lay off soon, hundreds maybe a thousand men. I don't want to be one of them.

WIFE
You work hard, they wont get rid of you.

BILLY
It's not like that. There's a lot of cheap labour around because of the state of the country and why should they pay me ten and six when they can get someone for five shillings dead to do exactly the same work.

WIFE
No!

BILLY
That's the way it is these days love. There's nothing we can do about it.

LIGHTS UP TO STREET AND WE SEE MEN LEAVING FOR WORK:

MAN
See you tonight!

MAN
Tarra kids. See you love.

WOMEN
Jack! Jack, ye' box! I made it up last night.

MAN
Thanks, darling. I couldn't 've got through the day without me butties!

WOMAN
See you our Mickey.

MAN
See you doll. See you after work.

WOMAN
Straight home now. Close your eyes as you pass the Castle and run while passing the Manor Arms, do you hear me? You might not get tempted.

MAN
I've tried love but it's the smell that gets me every time.

FRANCESCA
I will see you later my darling. It's good to see you smile again!

PAULI
It is working out. The job's great and the kids are settled.

FRANCESCA
Today I will write to Mama and tell her how good it is here in Birkenhead.

PAULI
Give her my love.

FRANCESCA
I will do, now you get to work….you don't want to be late.

KID
See you later daddy.

WOMAN
Don't work too hard!

MAN
I won't.

WOMAN
Go on….get out….ye' bloody nuisance!

MAN
See ye' love.

EVERYTHING GOES QUIET:

DOORS AGAIN START OPENING AND THE WOMEN GET ON WITH THEIR DAILY CHORES AS THE MEN SET ABOUT GOING TO WORK:

SONG 2: ROUTINE

Day after day, here we go again
Working in the yard with the same bunch of men
Nobody told us, It would be like this
Nobody cared to mention life wouldn't be bliss
Smell the smells all around
The dirt the muck and oil
Feel the sweat on your palms
From the hours of dirty toil
See the dangers around
We face them day to day
Somebody come and save me
Get me away

Day after day, the same routine
Doing the cooking and keeping everything clean
Nobody told us it'd be this way
Nobody mentioned this on our wedding day
Twenty four hours in a day
And I must work twenty three
Sorting things out for them all
But no one sorts it out for me
I break my back in the morning
And work all afternoon
Somebody come and save me
Come and save me soon

Week after week, that's how it goes
Keeping things all in order, keeping on my toes
Everyday passes by,
They roll into one
Must remember to enjoy myself –
One day we'll be gone
Sticking at it but we'll never be millionaires
We only just get by
Working at Lairds

MUSIC END:

SCENE FIVE

WOMEN ON THE STREET, AT THEIR DOORWAYS:

WOMAN
What's up chuck?

WOMAN
Your Clive 'been causing trouble again?

WOMAN
No it's not that….

WOMAN
He hasn't has he?

WOMAN
Hasn't what?

WOMAN
No….I don't believe it. Maureen Shuttlecock, I'd never have thought it!

WOMAN
Not in a million years.

WOMAN
But….

WOMAN
I tell you what, he's turning into a right 'you know what'….and I'll tell you something else for nothing, if he….you know….ever…. I mean, who is it for me to say, but, should he….and I don't mean the odd little diddly-dink, I mean the full Boer escapade…should he…. actually….I mean…. physically …..then without any shadow of a doubt - I'd give him what for, send him packing, ask for his what-jam-a-call it and don't give a monkeys uncle, second glance or a bit of how's ye father till pay day next week.

WOMAN
I'm with her!

WOMAN
But…he's not well, he's been off a week now – no pay, we're down to our last and he doesn't look like he's improving.

WOMAN
Poor sod.

WOMAN
Oh dear.

WOMAN
Such a lovely chap.

WOMAN
He's not allowed visitors and the doctor says he might have to go to the General.

WOMAN
Not allowed visitors.

WOMAN
No.

WOMAN
No!

WOMAN
He may be hospitalised

WOMAN
As well!

WOMAN
Yes.

WOMAN
Look at the time.

FIRST WOMAN LEAVES:

WOMAN
My oven's on – Stew again.

SECOND WOMAN LEAVES:

WOMAN
There's our Katy…Katy!

THIRD WOMAN LEAVES:

WOMAN
He might die.

WOMAN IS LEFT STANDING ALONE:

FRANCESCA
Are you alright?

WOMAN
I suppose so.

FRANCESCA
Would you like a cup of tea?

WOMAN
Yes.

FRANCESCA
I heard what you said and I'm sure your husband will be alright. They've got marvellous things in the new hospital,   they'll look after him there.

WOMAN
I know you're right but it doesn't help the house.

FRANCESCA
You bring your family here tonight for tea. Tomorrow we will go the priest.

SCENE SIX

LIGHTS UP ON LAIRDS MANAGEMENT MEETING:

MAN
This meeting is to discuss the plight of the workers at Lairds, this is due to the lack of monies needed. We will have to make cuts in the work force.

MAN
How will we tell the men at the yard that they won't be able to take home a wage? What will these men do for work?

MAN
I'm afraid that's not our problem.

MAN
We must look after our men.

MAN
We must look after ourselves and the future of Lairds itself.

MAN
We have no alternative than to take certain unskilled workers from the yard no matter how it affects them and their families.

MAN
There must be other ways top cut costs.

MAN
Once we've launched the sloops we'll be down to one project and that is not enough to hold a workforce of thousands in employment

MAN
There is no alternative.

MAN
There is only one solution…..

MAN
…..Cutbacks in the number of men on permanent employment.

MAN
And when work does start to build we will employ on a casual basis only – turn up and start work on a day to day basis….

MAN
…..giving the advantage of a cheaper workforce.

MAN
And thus attracting more profits for this great company!

MAN
Every cloud has a silver lining!

MAN
But what about our responsibility to the men?

MAN
They'll find other work, our problem is to try and keep the yard open.

MAN
I oppose this motion whole heartedly.

MAN
Aye.

MAN
Aye.

MAN
Aye.

MAN
Aye.

MAN
Settled. As from this point we will issue end of contracts to three thousand men.

MAN
You should give the respect they deserve and give them this news by word of mouth.

MAN
A representative is already on his way as we speak to the workers.

SCENE SEVEN

LIGHTS UP ON LADIES FLOWER ARRANGING

LADY
Edmund Kirby said his improvements would bring the Tranmere workhouse up to tip top shape.

LADY
I'm afraid, maybe the job was just too beyond the realms of conventional ideals.

LADY
The place is a state.

LADY
The place is disgusting.

LADY
The conditions are of a most primitive character.

LADY
It's degrading to the poor folk for whom life has dealt this unimaginable blow.

LADY
Oh Lydia, take a step back and calm down.

LADY
I have a girl who once stayed there….oh yes, she was a pitiful sight when I offered her a position - she cleans the lower quarters for me now – I feel I'm doing my bit at least!

LADY
But it's so inhumane.

LADY
And on our doorstep!

LADY
In the whole place, the whole place, I say…there is only one bathroom and that's used as a rough storage room for vegetables.

LADY
No!

LADY
No!

LADY
Yes. They say the only time they've heard of anyone bathing in it, was by a person suffering from a contagious complaint.

LADY
Contagious complaints!

LADY
In that place!

LADY
Yes.

LADY
Oh.

LADY
I vote in favour of passing the Tranmere Workhouse fit, beyond any reasonable apprehension, to house the poor, needy, suffering....

LADY
And contagious!

LADY
And contagious, and shall not require a visit from the upper Prenton Ladies Reform group for many years to come.

LADY
Seconded.

LADY
Thank the Lord!

SCENE EIGHT

LIGHTS UP ON 'YARD':

MAN:
I hear there's a couple of OBE's to be given out this week?

MAN
OBE's?

MAN
Will the queen be coming?

MAN
No! O…B…Es

MAN
Old brown envelopes. They give you the news before you open them! If you get given a brown envelope, you know you won't be in work the next week.

MAN
You're finished up.

MAN
There's no work for you.

MAN
At least it's polite.

MAN
Better then the D…C…M's

MAN
What's that?

MAN
It stands for 'don't come Monday'.

MAN
That's all they say….no thank you…no goodbye, just 'don't come Monday'!

MAN
There'll be a few of them as well.

MAN
Are things really that bad?

MAN
Who can say? The management could be telling the truth when they say we're a victim of our own success – building fine ships that will last forever or they may be attracted by the large stock of cheap labour around. Who knows?

MAN
We should stand up for ourselves.

MAN
We should stand up and be counted – they can't do this to their workforce.

MAN
They bloody well can and they bloody well are….and as for standing up for rights and wrongs or whatever, show me a man who'll try to twist the arm of the only real local employer and I'll show you a poor idiot with a sad wife and hungry children.

LIGHTS UP ON ARGYLE SHOW:

SONG 3: THE ARGYLE

Down at the old Argyle
Whether man, woman or child
You're bound to enjoy your night with us
We're just down your street
Ask anyone you meet
And we're handy for the trams or autobus.

Every night a different act

*From 'round the world and that's a fact
To entertain, amuse and educate
So go tell all your pals
You'll see fire and animals
Be sure to turn up early – don't be late*

*Oh it really is a treat and we've got a thousand seats
There's room to stretch your legs and have a laugh
Although it may seem quite a squash
Unless, of course, you're posh
So make sure before you turn up have a bath.*

*Our prices are quite cheap
Down on Argyle Street
You can see a show for a shilling, maybe more
So when you're feeling down
Down sit at home and frown
Come and change you ways and walk right through our door*

*Oh it really is a treat and we've got a thousand seats
There's room to stretch your legs and have a laugh
Although it may seem quite a squash
Unless, of course, you're posh
So make sure before you turn up have a bath.*

*You can hear the girlies laugh
After acts and that's a fact
You can hear the men folk whistle out for more
And at the end of every night
Not a dry eye there in sight
And there's always a chorus of encore!*

*The acts they will amaze
With their entertaining ways
They'll show you things you didn't know they'd do
And then you'll sit and gasp
At the end of every act
Rather stunned, I know I did – do you?*

*Oh it really is a treat and we've got a thousand seats
There's room to stretch your legs and have a laugh*

Although it may seem quite a squash
Unless, of course, you're posh
So make sure before you turn up have a bath.

LIGHTS SWITCH TO MAYOR:

MAYOR
Ladies and gentlemen, pray silence, for I have solemn news to deliver to you the people of Birkenhead. On this black day in our great nation's History, I regret to inform you of the death of our dearly beloved Queen, Victoria. The Queen is Dead, God save the King!

BACK TO MUSIC:

Oh it really is a treat and we've got a thousand seats
There's room to stretch your legs and have a laugh
Although it may seem quite a squash
Unless, of course, you're posh
So make sure before you turn up have a bath

SONG END:

LIGHTS UP ON CHARLIE CHAPLIN:

CHARLIE
Anyone who was anyone went to Birkenhead. The place was alive. The Argyle Theatre was the greatest theatre in the country for us lot, apart of course from the Palladium…that goes without saying. That was the route, you see. Get to Birkenhead and you know London wasn't far away. And what a crowd! What a crowd. They knew a good act when they saw one….and if they didn't like you, you certainly knew about it! We all knew the General wasn't too far….and we all knew the way!

CHARLIE EXITS.
LIGHTS DOWN:

SCENE NINE

LIGHTS UP ON STREET.THREE MEN ARE WALKING DOWN THE STREET AT NIGHT. IT IS CLEAR THEY'VE HAD A DRINK OR TWO:

MAN
The difference between a good woman and a fine beer is about three and six!

MAN
You don't know what you're saying man. Women have the hard work. My wife is up at four every morning sorting out the house and the food for the day…that's before I leave and the kids get up!

MAN
Aye, a woman's work is a hard day's graft.

MAN
We work hard ourselves lads!

MAN
Oh yes...to bring in the money.

MAN
That we do.

MAN
There's nothing like a hard days work.

MAN
Like the three of us did today!

MAN
Our working day consists of clocking in.

MAN
Clocking in.

MAN
Oh yes!

MAN
Building up a sweat....

MAN
It's very tiring.

MAN
Excruciatingly tiring!

MAN
By climbing over the wall and spending the morning in the Glass Barrel on dear old Market Street.

ALL
God bless her.

THEY LAUGH:

MAN
Come on lads. I beg to differ. The afternoon is spent discussion and deliberating in the Royal Castle or the Harp!

THEY LAUGH:

MAN
Then it's back over the wall and clocking off for which we'd receive a full day's wages, having spent the day sorting out the problems of the country and the questions of the universe....in the pub!

MAN
Now you can't say we spent all day in the pub. We spent at least fifteen minutes walking from one to another!

THEY ALL LAUGH:

CAMMELL
I set up business in Sheffield. Steel works. I did very well for myself, thank you very much. When the opportunity arose to become part of the greatest ship-builders in the world, I jumped at the chance. Steel works obviously compliment ship building with steel ships now being the only way to build. I was buying into a business as well as buying business for my own company. I couldn't lose! It was in recognition of my good nature and the quick deal that Cammell Lairds became Cammell Lairds and not Laird Cammells. Some did say that it would have sounded more like an exotic animals operation than ship builders if Mr Laird had got his way!

LIGHTS UP ON THE WOMEN MARCHING DOWN THE STREET:

WOMEN
We're going down the pub to get the men
They can't face the facts, so they've gone the pub again
It's always left to us to sort it out
So we're going down the pub to get the bastards out.
If there's any sign of trouble off they go
They think they know it all but they don't know
It's us who has to sort out what's for tea
To pay rent, pay the bills and keep the family.

WILLIAM LIONEL HITCHENS
I accept this position with great pride but also with sadness as we still mourn the great man, the late Chairman J. Macgregor Laird. Not only did he serve this company well, but he was the last Laird connected to the Yard. From 1824 through to 1910 the Lairds not only founded the company, but saw it through great times building it.

WOMEN
So we're going down the pub to get them out
They won't moan or fight with us – they won't shout
It's us who rule the roost - that they know
And if they don't sort this mess out then off they go.

41

WOMAN
Come on girls!

LIGHTS DOWN:
SFX:
LONE PLANE THEN GUNFIRE:

LIGHTS UP ON WILFRED OWEN:

OWEN
She said goodbye and he left her there,
Silent, caring, crying and unaware
That the next time they'd meet may be four or five years
While he fought the glorious war for her

Both trapped because of this evil that is around
One entrenched with bloody reminders, both sight and sound
The other aware that should he fail he'd never be found
And laid at rest, forever, in foreign ground.

The nights were dark in this pitiful war
The likes of which had never been seen before
Where hell rose up and opened its willing door
And witnessed by those who caused the endless gore

The pounding, sounding grinding from within
No one would, or could excuse this mortal sin
But he was there the times she thought of him
But only in death would they now be reunited

SILENCE:

SCENE TEN

APPRENTICE
I served me time after the war – I was too young to fight so I wasn't involved full on like, but we all felt it. There was a growing feeling of pride after it. Our men had done their bit….We were proud of them. I was proud of myself when I finished serving me

apprenticeship. We celebrated by going to Rossi's on Chester Street and spending the afternoon eating ice-cream! The work was good though…always kept changing in the yard. I played me part in building the Fullagar, the first all welded sea going vessel in the world! She was named after the engine which I thought was a shame. This was a world first it should have a name of some importance and some recognition of who we where and what we where – I would've called it the Cammell Laird, or the Birkenhead Glory, or Pride of the Town, but then I don't choose the names do I. We leave that to the important people – who knows one day they'll be naming buildings in Birkenhead after the Pyramids of Egypt! No I was only joking – that would never happen.

LIGHTS UP OUTSIDE LAIRD'S GATES:

MAN
I need to get picked today. I need the money, me little lads getting christened in a week and I need to pay for the do.

MAN
Don't build you hopes up.

MAN
Hope is all we can build at the moment.

MAN
Savage will give us work today – I'm sure of it.

MAN
Savvo will give us some work. I know him like, we used to work together on the same team, fitting. Good bloke, genuine, like.

MAN
I need this work today, we're going to get kicked out and the church can't help any more.

MAN
We've all got bills to pay, mate.

MAN
We all need the work.

MAN
But not all of us are going to get it, are we?

MAN
It'll go to the cheap labour.

MAN
There are no big contracts in, so the immigrants will get the work.

MAN
Bastards. Coming over here and taking our jobs.

MAN
Here's the Irish lot now.

A GROUP OF MEN, 'THE IRISH LOT', COME IN A STAND TO ONE SIDE, WAITING:

MAN
No dogs, no Blacks and no Irish used to be the signs – you'd see them everywhere, boarding houses and the like. No dogs, no Blacks and no Irish.

MAN
They're all over the place now.

MAN
Everywhere you turn there are a couple of Irish men having a laugh....

MAN
Singing.

MAN
Dying for a jig!

MAN
Taking our jobs.

MAN
Taking our money.

MAN
Taking our lives.

MAN
They work for buttons.

MAN
They'd work for potatoes, that lot. Birkenhead's heaven to them compared to barren lands of Ireland.

MAN
Shush, here's Savage now.

FOREMAN
If you could all stand in an orderly manner. Thank you men. We need platers, pipe-fitters, carpenters and welders today, the rest of you can come back tomorrow.

HALF THE MEN LEAVE:

FOREMAN
Now we'll have you, and you and you.

HE PICKS OUT A FEW MEN:

MAN
Picking the Irish again Savvo.

MAN
Cheap labour doesn't build ships it causes death.

MAN
How many drinks did he buy you last night.

FOREMAN
Quiet down. If you haven't been picked come back tomorrow.

MAN
What for? To find out who your friends are.

MAN
To watch a pathetic royal make decisions about decent men's lives.

MAN
Is he blue blooded?

MAN
No….a royal is one of the privileged in the yard – they talk to the bosses.

MAN
You're the scab on a sore on my arse Jack Savage. You're nothing but scum.

FOREMAN
Come here and say that Brown.

MAN
You're the lowest of the low, you're a traitor to your friends, the men who worked beside you for years when things where good. Now you wipe the backsides of those who click their fingers at you. You bow to those who you think are better. You've let yourself down mate, your not a Birkonian, you're a rat, a sewer rat.

FOREMAN
There's no need for that.

MAN
There's every need. Who was there when you need help you when you we're down? Families – we all pulled together. We didn't turn our back on you. You're a bastard Savage. I hope you and your family rot and burn in hell.

BROWN PUNCHES SAVAGE. THERE IS A SCUFFLE AND THE MEN ARE PULLED APART:

FOREMAN
You'll never work here again. Don't come back tomorrow. Don't come back ever, Brown. None of you come back. None of you.

THE FOREMAN IS LEFT ALONE CENTRE STAGE:

LIGHTS DOWN.

LIGHTS UP ON MEN WALKING DOWN STREET. THEY ARE JOINED BY THE FULL CAST.

MUSIC START:

SONG 4: BIRKENHEAD

I was born in Birkenhead
A great place where to start
I grew up in the town
And I worked down the yard
And the people that surrounded me
When things just got too hard
They loved me

I grew up in the times
When work was all we had
The sound of all around
Made life seem not so bad
And I worked hard at what I did
From the days I was a lad
I loved it

Feel the arms around me through the good times and the bad
Knowing what makes you happy and helping when you're sad
Knowing the people of this town will always make me smile
Knowing they looked out for me from the days I was a child

The times grew hard and work got less
The men numbered just a few
And our turn to be laid off
Was long time over due
When that day came I saw men cry

The biggest men I knew
We lost them

Feel the arms around me through the good times and the bad
Knowing what makes you happy and helping when you're sad
Knowing the people of this town will always make me smile
Knowing they looked out for me from the days I was a child

Feel the arms around me through the good times and the bad
Knowing what makes you happy and helping when you're sad
Knowing the people of this town will always make me smile
Knowing they looked out for me from the days I was a child
The big ship sails on the alley- alley-oh.

SONG END:

END OF ACT 1

ACT 2

SCENE ONE

MUSIC 'THE SOFT SATIN MOON'

LIGHTS UP ON WOMEN IN THE STREET:

WOMAN
The works coming in at the yard!

WOMAN
God save us all!

WOMAN
It's true. They've got a couple of big contracts.

WOMAN
Important ones at that.

WOMAN
So I hear – the Ark Royal no less.

WOMAN
The Lusitania!

WOMAN
It's the big one.

WOMAN
They'll be talking about Birkenhead again.

WOMAN
All around the world!

WOMAN
They'll be singing in Birkenhead again!

WOMAN
There'll be shopping as well.

WOMAN
Thank God for that!

WOMAN
And won't it be a blessing when the men go down the pub and get their miserable faces from under our feet!

WOMAN
I say to him – go on, spend your last pennies on a couple of pints, we'd all be happy then! But he says he wouldn't know anyone down there – none of the gang goes anymore.

WOMAN
My Charlie will be down there tonight and I might join him!

WOMAN
I may do myself.

WOMAN
We should all celebrate the smile they've put back on our faces.

WOMAN
The smile they've brought to Birkenhead!

WOMAN
Our town will live again!

WOMAN
Tonight through the bottom of a glass of brown ale!

MUSIC STARTS:

SONG 5: DRINK

Well drink, drink, drink, 'cause we bloody well can
We'll drink the town dry, we'll drink till we can't stand
We'll go down the Castle there's never much hassle
Or stop in the Harp for a lark
The Manor, Britannia, they won't understand ye'
The Old House At Home, or the Queens near the Park!

We'll drink, drink, drink, and we'll drink it well
We'll meet all our friends as we crawl from the Raglen Hotel
Then it's down to the Alex and on to the Imp
The Tranmere Park for half a drink
Head straight for the town The Fireman's is there
Then we'll fall into the Dock where things are a blur

We'll be drunk, drunk, drunk! And we don't care
We don't need drink we'll get drunk on the Birkenhead air!
But one for the road, that'll do fine
We'll see if we walk in a nice straight line
Pop in the Dragon and the Waterloo
Then, oh my word, what's in front of you!

Many a man has entered Skid row
And many a woman had prayed they'd never go
The walk from the Cally right up to the Barrel alone
Gives many a man the excuse not to go home

We'll be drunk drunk, drunk! And we don't care
We don't need drink we'll get drunk on the Birkenhead air!
But one for the road, that'll do fine
And we'll see if we walk in a nice straight line
The wife's going to have you seen the time
I shouldn't have had that last Aussie wine

We'll be drunk drunk, drunk! And we don't care
We don't need drink we'll get drunk on the Birkenhead air!
But one for the road, that'll do fine
And we'll see if we walk in a nice straight line
The wife's going to have you seen the time
I shouldn't have had that last Aussie wine
'cause we're drunk!

MUSIC END:

LIGHTS UP ON WORKER:

MAN
I said to them, let our lads go…we'll get the bugger up! 'No, leave it to us', they said, 'Let us do the work, it's ours now'! Would you

credit it? I couldn't believe it….so many lives. It was on tests. We let it go to them but we had our lads on it! No one could've predicted what happened…but we could've worked out how to get those lads up. They wouldn't let us – their men were trained. There was no excuse for it. Red tape, white papers – what ever it was they had to do it themselves. It took days for their team to get there, just off Anglesey….days. We could've been there in under three hours. We could've sorted it out. When we heard we all got together and worked out what was the best plan – we came up with the perfect rescue solution. But that was blocked immediately by the powers that be….blocked. The Thetis it was called.

LIGHTS DOWN:

LIGHTS UP ON NAVAL OFFICER ON THE PHONE:

NAVAL
Sir, I regret to inform you, the Thetis has gone down. Ninety-nine men, lost sir. We did all that we possibly could, I can assure you. Ninety-nine, sir….Dead.

SILENCE:

SCENE TWO

AIR RAID SIRENS:

LIGHTS OUT AND PEOPLE SCRAMBLING FOR SHELTERS:

LIGHTS UP ON CHURCHILL:

CHURCHILL
Do not let us speak of darker days: Let us speak rather of sterner days. These are not dark days; these are great days – the greatest days our country has ever lived; and we must all thank God that we have been allowed, each of us according to our stations, to play a part in making these days memorable in the history of our race.

LIGHTS UP ON STREET:

ONE OF THE HOUSES IN THE STREET IS JUST A PILE OF RUBBLE:

ENTER KIDS:

KID
Friggin' hell! Hey, our Jack, look here. The Jones' have left. They've taken everything – even the house.

KID
No, quiet Micky – that's been hit!

KID
NO!

KID
Yes – Old Mr Jones was still in there, the rest had made it to the Anderson.

KID
How's old Mr Jones now?

KID
They haven't got him out yet

KID
Why not?

KID
He was last seen on the top floor, now he's definitely in the cellar – they reckon there's no hope for him. He's dead.

KID
Jones…dead!

KID
Yes

KID
Wow. It all happens round here doesn't it?

KID
Because of the yard.

KID
What?

KID
Adolf wants rid of Lairds – their ships are too good for his lot, that's what me dad said.

ENTER OTHER KIDS:

KID
Hi.

KID
Hi

KID
What the frig has happened there?

KID
The Jones' was hit last night.

KID
We felt it.

KID
Anyone dead?

KID
Hundreds

KID
Only old Mr Jones.

KID
Get away.

KID
Yeah.

KID
I wish we had bombs in our street.

KID
Yeah, we don't even get milkmen.

KID
Once they've finished we can go and look for bits.

KID
Shrapnel

KID
Bullets

KID
Bodies.

KID
Gerrrrrrmans!

THEY ALL LOOK HORRIFIED:

KID
No there won't be, will there?

KID
Gary Falmer from Duke Street says they found three Germans a couple of weeks back. Mr. Falmer held them prisoner in the outside privy till the home guard turned up – They were in there for at least an hour.

KID
Did he get to speak to them?

KID
Oh aye, yeah. He tried but they talked double Dutch.

KID
Aren't they on our side?

KID
They gave him two bullets and a Nazi badge.

KID
No!

KID
Oh yeah – I've seen them….I touched a Nazi badge.

KID
Traitor.

KID
You're only jealous.

KID
What did it look like then.

KID
German.

KID
Let's go and see what we can find!

LIGHTS DOWN.

AGAIN A SIREN IS HEARD:

CHURCHILL
We must continue in the spirit this country has been proud to bear witness to and hold for centuries. We must hold firm and continue our work for this great nation we must fight on with our heads firmly high.

SCENE THREE

BACK ON THE STREET. THE WOMEN ARE LINING THE ROAD WAITING FOR THE KING GEORGE VI AND QUEEN ELIZABETH TO ARRIVE TO INSPECT THE DAMAGE AND MEET THE PEOPLE:

ACTION MOVES FROM WOMEN TO WOMEN:

WOMAN
I've been here for two hours. I'm starting to freeze.

WOMAN
Oh….they're worth the wait.

WOMAN
You think they'd be on time.

WOMAN
You think they'd make the effort to get here early on a day like this.

WOMAN
They won't be long now.

WOMAN
I'll give them another half hour.

WOMAN
It's bordering on ignorant.

WOMAN
Disgraceful.

WOMAN
Do you mind…we're at war! Statements like that could be seen as treason against the crown. Now stop your moaning or take it somewhere else.

WOMAN
Always been above herself that Margaret Shackleton. Always been a toffee nosed cow.

WOMAN
I know. And she never rinses her nets!

TWO OTHER WOMEN:

WOMAN
Flat out they're working. Flat out. Mr Hitler and his lot are going to have to think again. Birkenhead's going to win this war for this country.

WOMAN
That's the feeling down the yard. They're averaging a launch every twenty days.

WOMAN
Every twenty days! That's unbelievable.

WOMAN
All fighting ships.

WOMAN
Undeniably outstanding.

WOMAN
The men are determined to do their bit.

WOMAN
They want to make their mark in the war effort – '*it's not front line but it's as important,*' my Arthur says.

WOMAN
Vera Kennedy in number six hasn't heard from her Bobby for three months. She's up the wall!

WOMAN
We're lucky in a way, having ours home, knowing where they are….and that. I know the Germans have been giving us a good hiding but we're still with them.

TWO OTHER WOMEN:

WOMAN
This is their second visit; they came to visit bomb sites in August as well.

WOMAN
I know….I missed the first one. I was tied up in the front bedroom having our Alice. My word she was a struggle. I couldn't get out of bed till that afternoon with her. The others were fine….I just dropped them out and got on with it….no, you can't feel sorry for yourself in childbirth.

WOMAN
It so good of them to come and support their people.

TWO OTHER WOMEN:

WOMAN
They say the bombing's going to get worse!

WOMAN
You're going to have to learn to move faster then

WOMAN
We're all right with our shelter.

WOMAN
I use the big one near us in Tranmere.

WOMAN
I've heard it's nice there.

WOMAN
Well it's not Buckingham palace and it's certainly not home!

WOMAN
Nice…

WOMAN
I like the Stations. I feel you always feel safe in a tunnel with a ready supply of Cadbury's from a machine,

TWO OTHER WOMEN:

WOMAN
Oooh...I think I see something.

WOMAN
The Queen is so beautiful.

WOMAN
Oh she is.

WOMAN
She does this country proud.

THERE IS EXCITEMENT IN THE CROWN AS THE CAR DRIVES CLOSER: HEADS FOLLOW IT QUICKLY PAST AND THE EXCITEMENT WAINS:

WOMAN
Wasn't she gorgeous?

WOMAN
I feel privileged.

WOMAN
Didn't she look beautiful?

WOMAN
Yeah....beautiful.

WOMAN
Well that's made my day!

TWO OTHER WOMEN:

WOMAN
Have they passed?

WOMAN
Just.

WOMAN
Well bloody hell….I stand here for two hours and the moment I need to rub me corns and release some pressure on me feet….they pass!

WOMAN
They'll be back – we haven't seen the last of the Luftwaffe yet.

THE WOMEN CHEER AND FREEZE:

SIRENS:

LIGHTS ON CHAIRMAN, WAR BLITZ COMMITTEE:

CHAIRMAN
The Raids continued; they were heavy around Christmas 1940 but the town's worst raid came on the night of the 12/13th March 1941 when in a murderous eight hours 288 people were killed.

SOME OF THE WOMEN LEAVE THE TABLEAUX:

40 Land mines were dropped….

MORE WOMEN LEAVE STAGE:

….and 180 heavy bombs were dropped over a large area of Birkenhead.

MORE WOMEN LEAVE STAGE:

The scene in Birkenhead the next morning was of grim devastation.

BACK TO STREET. A WOMAN IS STANDING ALONE AS:

KID
Mrs Jackson, is your Albert coming out to play?

SHE DOES NOT ANSWER:

KID
Mrs Jackson?

SHE DOES NOT ANSWER:

KID
Mrs Jackson!

MAN
Lad, many houses were hit round here last night, including the Jackson's.

KID
But where's Albert?

MAN
They haven't found him yet…..but they're looking.

KID
Albert?

MAN
Go home son.

KID
But Mister.

SILENCE:

SONG 6: SOMEONE LIGHT A CANDLE

Someone light a candle, someone say a prayer.
Someone say what love is when nobody is there.
Someone then said something, someone made me cry.
Someone whispered nothing, then I wondered why.

Tell me where my heart is, tell me who knows
Ask me silly questions that no one else will know.
Give me no solutions, Let no one through my door.
'Cause no one knows my password
No one's been there before.

Someone light a candle, someone say a prayer.
Someone say what love is, but nobody is there.
Someone then said something, someone made me cry.
Someone whispered nothing, then I wondered why.

Who am I to object to you, who am I to care.
Who am I to argue when no one else is there.
Question after question spinning round my head,
   Hating someone close to you
   Or a love affair instead.

Someone light a candle, someone say a prayer.
Someone say what love is, but nobody is there.
Someone then said something, someone made me cry,
   Someone whispered nothing,
Then I wondered, Then I wondered, Then I wondered, why?

MUSIC END

SCENE FOUR

JOHNSON
I would like to announce, in my second year of office, that Cammell Laird shall now be known as Cammell Laird and Co (Ship Builders and Engineers)

THE END TABLEUAX TURNS AND PLACARDS ARE RAISED AS IN A PICKET LINE:

MAN
Get of your arses and tell us what's going on!

MAN
Get your cheque books out.

MAN
Show us your money!

MAN
We know you're earning a fortune on this one - Share it!

MAN
Come out and talk.

MAN
Show us some respect.

MAN
Talk to us.

MAN
We don't want to hear about losses.

MAN
No profit.

MAN
There just the usual management moans.

MAN
Start talking.

MAN
Put your money where your mouth is.

MAN
We're not going to back down.

MAN
We know the deal and you've got to share it out amongst the men.

ALL
SHARE IT! SHARE IT! SHARE IT!

THE PICKET LINE FREEZES. THREE WOMEN:

WOMAN
They're up the wall. They don't know what the management position is.

WOMAN
Very comfortable, I'm sure.

WOMAN
They won't give in. A shilling an hour. It's not a lot.

WOMAN
It'll only put them in line with other tradesmen in the yard.

WOMAN
Disgusting.

WOMAN
They're not letting up though.

WOMAN
There's talk that the whole yard will come out behind them.

WOMAN
And so they should.

ALL
SHARE IT! SHARE IT! SHARE IT!

THE PICKET LINE FREEZES WITH HAND UP IN THE AIR AND SILOUETTES A BEATLE AUDIENCE. SPOTLIGHT ON ANNOUNCER:

ANNOUNCER
Please give a warm welcome to The Beatles.

SCREAMS. LIGHTS ON JOHN LENNON TALKING DOWN A MICROPHONE:

LENNON
Well this is a fab hall. I didn't know Birkenhead Technical College was so big – mind you, you're going to need all the workers you can down at the yard. This one's for all those who are working on the submarines in town where you were born – there's a song in there somewhere. Here we go lads, one…two…three…

LIGHTS BACK ON PICKET LINE:

MAN
Help – we don't need help! We're going to fight for this one men. We're going to show the royals that we won't stand for being taken for idiots! We're going to stand up for what we want, for what we deserve. What do we want? We want at least a shilling an hour, per man. Shipwrights should be paid at the same rate as other trades in the yard and we're going to see that happen. A shilling – that's nothing on this contract – they've been give an blank cheque for both the Revenge and the Renown, a blank cheque that should be paying for our time, over time and more work for us all.

ALL
SHARE IT! SHARE IT! SHARE IT!

PICKET LINE FREEZES AS IF IT'S A NIGHT OUT IN THE PUB. LIGHTS UP ON MEN IN PUB:

MAN
We'll stand together on this one. We'll fight together and we'll win together.

MAN
And we'll stand together all the way.

MAN
Continue the strike.

MAN
Careful men – This strike might not be your doing?

MAN
What?

MAN
What the hell's he talking about?

MAN
You'll be the scapegoats if things go wrong.

MAN
You'll end up with the blame if things go wrong.

LIGHTS ON APPRENTICE:

APPRENTICE
They wouldn't let us support the men. Apprentices don't strike… *"Get back to work."* We had to work in the Pneumatic Department while they stood their ground. They all understood, but it was still uncomfortable for us. There were four of us. Weir, Harry Minor bird, Flockhead and myself. We would sit and discuss the situation at every possible moment. We wanted to show our support. We were part of the team…part or the yard, like. Anyway, we decided that one of us should go and tell the management, Yellow Joe, what we felt. Weir suggested we draw straws and we all agreed. I drew first….fine. Minor bird was shitting himself, you could see. He was never one to complain or stand up to anyone….we all knew why….we'd met his mother. But he was safe…long straw. Weir too was safe and Flockhead drew the short one. Poor Flockhead, but he didn't seem to mind. We watched him climb the step and go inside the manager's office. Literally two seconds passed then we heard an almighty '*WHAT*' from the office. Yellow Joe stormed out dragging Flockhead by the ear, behind him. We all ran back to our work. We thought we were in for it. Talk about standing up for our rights! We could hardly stand – our legs were like jelly as Yellow Joe marched towards us with his catch dragging behind him. *"Do you want to go home?"* he asked each of us individually and, like any man would in defiant circumstances, we all said *"no"*, and left poor Flockhead to take the rap. He was suspended for two week on no pay.

BACK TO MEN:

MAN
They want to bring in new labour.

MAN
They need specialist skills.

MAN
They're looking for a way to do this, an excuse, a reason.

MAN
You're not doing yourself any favours.

MAN
Things could blow up in your faces.

MAN
Things are going to change on the yard.

MAN
Better?

MAN
Things have never been good for the workers.

MAN
Things have to change.

MAN
Shipbuilding is a dirty business and the general standards of cleanliness and precision are at odds with more precise requirements of nuclear engineering.

MAN
We all should be concerned.

MAN
We need new contracts.

MAN
Better wages.

ALL
SHARE IT! SHARE IT! SHARE IT!

BACK TO STREET:

WOMAN
It's looking bad.

WOMAN
It's looking good.

WOMAN
Things will never be the same.

WOMAN
My George says there's trouble if we lose this contract.

WOMAN
Our Paul thinks if they don't lose this contract there's going to be trouble.

WOMAN
There's word of more work.

WOMAN
More workers.

WOMAN
Outsiders!

WOMAN
Imagine that, outsiders coming into Lairds!

WOMAN
John Laird will be turning in his grave!

WOMAN
They need more skilled labour.

WOMAN
Birkenhead hasn't got it.

WOMAN
Not near enough.

WOMAN
…If at all.

WOMAN
We can't knock the men!

WOMAN
Our men.

WOMAN
It's a struggle for them.

WOMAN
No one knows.

WOMAN
What's happening!

WOMAN
What's going on!

WOMAN
They need to sit on the hands and let those upstairs pull their apron strings and make decisions.

WOMAN
The only decisions that lot can make is whether to see the dessert trolley or not!

ALL
SHARE IT! SHARE IT! SHARE IT!

LAIRDS BOARDROOM:

MAN
This strike has been going on for long enough. We are now confident we can continue with work on the first vessel and the start of the second. The men are happy and it is time to introduce more workers in the yard. , we are back in business and have over eleven thousand workers at this present time! I suggest that since, for the next year, the company seeks a smaller merchant ship programme to allow for an all out effort on Polaris. Naval contracts of this kind are the future of shipbuilding. Submarines are the future of warfare and protection. Cammell Laird will once again be the greatest ship

builder in the world at the forefront of this particular skill. God Save the Queen!

CHEERS AS THE CROWD FILLS THE STREET:

WOMAN
Did you see it?

MAN
Oh yes!

WOMAN
Back on top.

MAN
We're the greatest again.

WOMAN
The Greatest.

MAN
The best.

MAN
It all started here.

WOMAN
And rightly has returned home!

MAN
Where it belongs.

WOMAN
The whole country should be proud

WOMAN
I heard the whole town scream.

MAN
It's the greatest time for all of us.

WOMAN
The whole world is pointing our direction.

MAN
And Geoff Hurst is the man who sealed it.

WOMAN
They think it's all over….

LIGHTS DOWN:

SCENE FIVE

SONG 7: SOFT SATIN MOON

Life is grand girls
Walking the streets at night
Avoiding all the light
From the soft satin moon

Take my hand girls
Things have never been so right
Walking through the night
In the soft satin moon

We know the streets
We know the men
We see them all come back again
And on this road
We know the code

Don't know the ships
Don't know the strangers
But we recognise the dangers
Corporation road
We've found our home

Life is good girls
The work is plentiful
Enough for us all

In our soft satin gowns

You can smile girls
They'll always need our sort
Even when the money's short
In our soft satin gowns

We know the streets
We know the men
We see them all come back again
And on this road
We know the code

Don't know the ships
Don't know the strangers
But we recognise the dangers
Corporation road
We've found our home

Life is grand girls
Walking the streets at night
Avoiding all the lights
From the soft satin moon

SONG END:

BACK TO DAYLIGHT:

LAD
I want to be a hippie.

GIRL
My uncle Dylan's a hippie….He wears flowery shirts and smokes weeds.

LAD
Eeeeh. Does he wet the bed?

GIRL
It wouldn't matter if he did. He sleeps outside under the stars with his friends.

LAD
What!

GIRL
He's got a lovely big house in Oxton and chooses to spend his nights outside.

LAD
Cool.

GIRL
Strange.

LAD
With it.

GIRL
….And he listens to music with his eyes closed and moves his head like this.

SHE IMITATES MOVING HER HEAD FROM SIDE TO SIDE:

LAD
Groovy

GIRL
Yeah, he told us once he and his friends sat naked in Birkenhead Park all through the night

LAD
Peace man.

GIRL
No one bothered them. They sat there all night looking at the stars and talking about life.

LAD
With no clothes on?

GIRL
Yeah.

LAD
Wow!

PAUSE:

LAD
Do you fancy coming down the Arno and trying that hippie thing with me.

GIRL
Get away will ye'. You're a bloody pervert.

LAD
No I'm not, I'm a hippie, now get them off.

THEY LAUGH:

ENTER LAD:

LAD
Alright you two, what are you up to?

GIRL
Just chatting.

LAD
Great.

LAD
You look grotty.

GIRL
Yeah really grotty.

LAD
I know. Me mam's not been the baggy for ages – we're skint. Me dad's been laid off hasn't me.

GIRL
From the yard.

LAD
Yeah.

LAD
Me dad said there's work there for years. We've got a catalogue and everything.

GIRL
Yeah, we have, and the Provvo. That's why I look all done up like.

LAD
No. Me dad's been out two weeks now – and it doesn't look like he's going back.

LAD
There'll be more submarines.

GIRL
Soon.

LAD
I hope so!

LAD
World warfare has changed so much. Submarines are our future and the yard is at the forefront.

GIRL
Has your dad been spouting off again?

LAD
No. That's what they've been saying for years.

LAD
It looks like they where wrong. It looks like the work's dried up.

GIRL
Blimey!

SCENE SIX

LIGHTS UP ON MANAGEMENT MEETING:

MAN
The goose that had laid our golden egg has flown, gentlemen. The government has turned its back on the yard.

MAN
Preposterous.

MAN
It's a disgrace!

MAN
We should fight it.

MAN
There's very little we can do. We need the government on our side to keep things going here.

MAN
But with them announcing that all future business for the construction of nuclear submarines would be placed at Barrow without any competitive tender, we're up the river!

MAN
We're in deep trouble.

MAN
The end could be in sight for the yard.

MAN
The subs were our future. We know what we've been doing for the last few years but then there wasn't an end of this work in sight.

MAN
They said it was the future.

MAN
They said it was our future.

MAN
If we'd have known we could have put things in place.

MAN
....Training, updating of skills for the building of cruisers, liners and the like. That's big business around the world but we don't have the skills to compete anymore.

MAN
We should've seen in coming, been prepared.

MAN
But they promised us this work, this ongoing work.

MANAGING DIRECTOR
Gentlemen, this time has come very suddenly. The bottom has dropped out of everything, and no one was left looking around saying where's my next order coming from? You've got all these men in the yard. What on earth are we going to do? We are very disappointed. When we took on the Polaris we where given to understand that there would be follow-on nuclear orders and we were prepared to take it, because we thought there would be a follow on.

MAN
We are not to blame.

MAN
We trusted what we were being told.

MAN
If you can't trust the Ministry of Defence....

PAUSE:

LIGHTS DOWN:

SCENE SEVEN

BACK ON STREET:

WOMAN
The market's gone.

WOMAN
What?

WOMAN
No!

WOMAN
Didn't you hear the commotion last night? It was Birkenhead. Fire.

WOMAN
Not the market!

WOMAN:
Yes…ablaze…you could see the flames from Rock Ferry to Wallasey pool. All of it destroyed.

WOMAN
What are we going to do?

WOMAN
Where are we going to go?

WOMAN
Liverpool.

WOMAN
I'm not going over there to do me shopping.

WOMAN
It's not right going to Liverpool to do your market shopping.

WOMAN
You go to Liverpool for your posh stuff.

WOMAN
From George Henry Lee's.

WOMAN
You wouldn't be allowed in the place.

WOMAN
Or Lewis's and Blackler's, but not your Market shopping.

WOMAN
That's what Birkenhead Market's for.

WOMAN
But now it's gone.

WOMAN
The heart of the town.

WOMAN
Where am I going to get me nets now?

WOMAN
Or me cheap cigarettes?

WOMAN
Nowhere else could you buy yellow fish.

WOMAN
Or replacements for any smashed dish.

WOMAN
I'm not going to Rostance's for me toys.

WOMAN
And what about lunch for the boys?

WOMAN
We're going to have to make do with town.

WOMAN
Now that Birkenhead Market's burnt down!

WOMAN
I've never worried about winkles before.

WOMAN
For Cockles now you'll need Moreton shore.

WOMAN
What about books for me gran?

WOMAN
Where else can I buy half a lamb?

WOMAN
Me frillies and me cheap high class shoes!

WOMAN
School uniforms – call the Birkenhead News!

WOMAN
What about little knick-knacks?

WOMAN
And spuds that come in the sack.

WOMAN
Christmas will be expensive this year.

WOMAN
Now that Birkenhead Market's not there!

LADIES EXIT:

SCENE EIGHT:

ENTER CLEANING LADY AND GOVERNMENT OFFICIAL:

MRS SMITH
I didn't know what to say and where to put myself when the asked me. It was a first, a memorable milestone the director said. I Ellen Smith, office cleaning supervisor and the yards longest serving female employee....have been asked to launch a ship.

OFFICIAL
We intend to continue to support Birkenhead's shipyard and will finance the yards facilities....

MRS SMITH
It's a bulk carrier and I've got the responsibility of smashing the bottle against the side of it. My family are so proud of me!

OFFICIAL
....culminating in the erection of a covered construction hall 147 metres long and 107 metres wide.

MRS SMITH
The Oakwood. That's what it's called and it's a bulk carrier. I don't mind – it's not the Queen Mary but it's my ship and I'm going to launch it.

OFFICIAL
And 50 metres high. This facility will be completed by 1978 and is a symbol of the belief this government has in the Birkenhead yard and Cammell Laird as world class shipbuilders.

MRS SMITH
I was nervous, very nervous. I thought to myself, all I have to do is break a bottle…and there we have it….launched. But, no, I was still so nervous.

OFFICIAL
I also see the nationalisation of the company as part of British Shipbuilders and with a reduced, yet strong workforce congratulate the yard on securing contracts for three type 42 warships.

MRS SMITH
I did it though. *I name this ship The Oakwood. May she sail well and all who sail aboard her.* Then I smashed the bottle – seemed a bit of a waste – it would've gone done nice with a Sunday roast, but not to worry.

OFFICIAL
Long live Cammell Laird and God Save the Queen.

SCENE NINE:

LIGHTS UP ON DOLE QUEUE:

MAN
What are they frightened of? Why on earth do they put themselves behind a glass screen. We're just men signing on.

MAN
They think they're the direct link to number ten.

MAN
It's Callaghan's money they're passing over.

MAN
They think they're responsible.

MAN
It's what they think of us that I'm worried about. I've worked hard all me life. Yes, there have been a few times when I've been out of work, but not for long. This place though, makes you feel it's your own fault. It's your problem and you need to sort it out.

CLERK
Next please.

MAN
It degrades you.

MAN
Makes you feel like scum.

MAN
We shouldn't have been laid off in the first place.

MAN
The whole thing stinks – there was plenty of work for all of us.

MAN
There should be an enquiry into how the yard's being managed. It should investigate top management and unions.

CLERK
Next please.

MAN
That's the problem – workers are blaming the management and the management are blaming the Government.

MAN
Why have they laid off most of the workforce – so fast?

MAN
That's nearly 4000 men.

MAN
There's something going on.

CLERK
Next please.

MAN
They shouldn't have taken the £2 off us.

MAN
Disagreement – it's about no one knowing who's saying what.

MAN
450 on unofficial strike – 4000 laid off. You can't say there's nothing fishy going on.

CLERK
Next please.

SCENE TEN:

LIGHTS UP ON JUBILEE KIDS:

KID
I've waited for this day for ages.

KID
June the 2nd 1977!

KID
Jubilee Day.

KID
Street Party Day!

AS ACTION HAPPENS A TABLE GETS SET:

MOTHER
Get your face washed. I don't want the neighbours talking.

FATHER
I'm just popping out to pick up the beer.

MOTHER
Any excuse!

KID
We're playing games.

KID
We're having a big table that stretches from one end of the street to the other.

KID
There are parties all over town.

KID
They're blocking the end of streets of with chairs, tables, wardrobes, everything!

KID
Everyone will be partying on the streets today.

KID
But ours is going to be the best!

KID
Fountain Street's got a band playing!

KID
We've got pass the parcel.

KID
Upper Brassey Street's got clowns and a mini circus.

KID
There's balloons all down Argyle Street South. Red white and blue.

MOTHER
We've got balloons.

MOTHER
Get Blowing kids!

MOTHER
What are they going to do on Rodney Street? That's not a street it's a mountain.

KID
Where's the food.

KID
We did the cheese butties.

KID
We made Jelly.

KID
Me mum wouldn't let me do anything. She says I'm a nibbler.

KID
We did the pork pies.

KID
I put silver foil round fifteen grapefruit halves.

KID
And I speared the cheese and pineapple.

KID
It's going to be a great day!

KID
All for our queen.

KID
God Save the Queen!

MOTHER
Right kids, Grab a chair.

THE PARTY BEGINS. DIALOGUE AS PARTY HAPPENS:

MOTHER
You behave yourselves and don't show me up in front of the neighbours.

MOTHER
Marty, stop putting your fingers in the Jelly.

MOTHER
Roll your sleeves up Andrew. Use a handkerchief in future.

KID
Are these serviettes or napkins?

MOTHER
They're napkins round here and serviettes in Heswall.

MOTHER
Kevin, pull your trousers back up and leave Lucy alone.

FATHER:
Beers up lads!

FATHER
Pass us a party pack and tin opener.

FATHER
You'll never get that open dry!

MOTHER
Who's burst this space hopper?

MOTHER
Don't you be blaming our Michael, Thomas or Luke. They were sat over here.

MOTHER
It's always that lot.

KID
Mum there's no chicken legs left.

KID
The ice cream's melting.

KID
Mary Jones has wet herself.

MOTHER
Mary, get inside now.

MOTHER
Keep it clean.

MOTHER
Has anyone got a towel?

MOTHER
…On the landing, my house. The door's open.

KID
I'm full

KID
I feel sick.

KID
I've been sick.

KID
Twice!

EVERYONE TURNS AND CHEERS:

MAN
Ladies and Gentlemen, your first female Prime Minister, the right honourable Margaret Thatcher.

THATCHER
We are happy to lead this country confidently and vehemently through the next five years and beyond. We shall introduce a denationalisation programme that will revolutionise British Industry as we know it. There shall be no more us and them, management and union, it'll be the man on the street who will be responsible for his own pennies in his pocket. It will be the industries themselves who will be responsible for their own pockets, filling them as well as spending and it'll be every man for himself and his family.

SCENE ELEVEN:

TWO WOMEN:

WOMAN
We've bought our own house.

WOMAN
Go away. How did you manage that?

WOMAN
Everybody's doing it.

WOMAN
I don't know. I rent, me mother rents, me granny rents and theirs before them. It doesn't seem right.

WOMAN
If it doesn't seem right then why is the council selling the houses then?

WOMAN
No!

WOMAN
Yes.

WOMAN
No.

WOMAN
It's the 'New' Britain. Everyone has the right to climb on the property ladder. Listen to Maggie.

WOMAN
But I haven't got the money.

WOMAN
You don't need money to buy a house. You need a mortgage.

WOMAN
Oh I don't want to go into debt.

WOMAN
A mortgage isn't debt, it's investment. My bank manager has made a special deal for me. He's given me an endowment.

WOMAN
That's disgusting.

WOMAN
No….You borrow a pot of money off one lot of people, then you pay back the interest while giving another lot of people money to play with. After twenty five years you get a lump sum to pay back the people who lent you the money in the first place.

WOMAN
That's complicated.

WOMAN
That's not all. And there may be some money left over – thousands that goes straight into you back pocket.

WOMAN
That's nice!

WOMAN
It can't fail.

WOMAN
Sounds brilliant.

PAUSE:

WOMAN
Unless of course when they play with your money and they don't win.

WOMAN
What happens then?

WOMAN
At the end of twenty five years you owe everyone money and you don't own your house.

WOMAN
Nasty.

WOMAN
But the chances of that happening....

MUSIC - 'CANDLE':
MAN STANDS 'LOOKING OUT TO SEA':

MAN
They're there
We know they're there.
But where?
They know.
The other side in this escapade.
The governments of two countries fighting,
Killing men.
Who stands where?
But at least they know they're there.
The Birkenhead vessels lie beneath the waves
With the capability of sending thousands to their graves
Quietly lying waiting as a threat.
To see how far they'll go or close they'll get.
The enemy worries at what the can do

They're there
They know they're there.
We Know
Our men hold the British land
While the top brass do what they can.
Men die
People worry
But at least we know they're there
Laird's subs lie undeterred.
Undetected in the ice cold sea
Helping the Falklands become, once again free.

SCENE TWELVE:

MANAGERS MEETING:

MAN
Good news gentlemen. We've been designated by the E.C. as a warship building yard.

MAN
Great news.

MAN
At last we're being recognised again.

MAN
We've been waiting for this.

MAN
Once again Cammell Lairds' is back on top.

MAN
This does however have one drawback. We will be denied access to the S.I.F.

MAN
The Shipbuilding Intervention Fund.

MAN
Which means we won't be subsidised in the building of merchant ships.

MAN
Liners.

MAN
Ferries.

MAN
Anything but warships.

MAN
But we've built the best in the world.

MAN
We've made our name building some of the greatest ships in history.

MAN
No more. Without equal subsidies other shipbuilders will be offering cheaper tenders.

MAN
We've been put in an awkward situation.

MAN
There is nothing we can do.

MAN
Can we not change our warship designation?

MAN
If that were to happen the European Commission may ask for some of the 140million European aid back.

MAN
This has, in effect, sealed the fate of this yard.

MAN
…And eight others in this country.

MAN
Sacrificed.

MAN
Ludicrous!

MAN
Ridiculous.

MAN
Who on earth accepted this aid package?

MAN
It came from number 10.

MAN
From the PM.

SCENE THIRTEEN:

TWO LADS ON STREET CORNER:

LAD
Alright mate.

LAD
Alright.

LAD
How's it going, like?

LAD
Oh Yeah, sound as.

LAD
Nice one.

LAD
Do you want any stuff mate?

LAD
Yeah, I'm nearly out – the girlfriend's been dipping.

LAD
Trouble?

LAD
Nah.

LAD
Fifteen quid, an eighth

LAD
Sound.

LAD
You can get all sorts of stuff round here you know, if you ever want to try something different.

LAD
No thanks, I'm a bit short – I haven't cashed me giro and the boss won't pay me till the end of the week.

LAD
Use your housing.

LAD
That gets paid straight to the landlord after I got kicked out of me last place.

LAD
Why was that?

LAD
I kept spending me dosh on weed.

LAD
Oh Aye. Sound.

SCENE FOURTEEN:

WOMEN ON STREET:

WOMAN
Your Mike back in work yet?

WOMAN
No he's back in the pub. He spends more time there than he does in our house.

WOMAN
Same with my Terry. Soon as he gets his hands on any money it's off to the pub.

WOMAN
I don't know how we get by.

WOMAN
I wouldn't get by without me book.

WOMAN
They've given me money for a new cot, bedding and clothes for the little one.

WOMAN
Must've been nice spending that.

WOMAN
I didn't spend it; it went straight down the Cross with him. He came home rotten that night. We'll get by though.

WOMAN
Our Steve's got a little job on the side.

WOMAN
You want to watch he doesn't get caught.

WOMAN
No one gets caught.

WOMAN
Him at 23 got caught – has to pay the lot back.

WOMAN
Doesn't seem right.

WOMAN
It's the only way to live these days. You can't afford to live on what you get.

WOMAN
They have to have a job on the side to get by.

WOMAN
Who'd buy the Christmas presents?

WOMAN
Who'd pay for the telly license?

WOMAN
Who'd pay for the car?

WOMAN
Who'd pay for the holiday?

WOMAN
No, these days if you're unemployed, you've got to work to make ends meet.

WOMAN
Half the town's doing it.

SONG 8: UNEMPLOYMENT:

Look into my eyes
And see the soul behind my smile
It's honest and it's true
But what you get's in front of you

No one tells us how we feel
I'm out of work and my life's not real
Getting through an empty day
Just wastes a life away

I will try
To keep this smile upon my face

We'll get by
But signing on's no saving grace
'cause you see
My own pride's a part of me
When it's gone
What's the point in going on
Today
Tomorrow
We all know that it's true
What else can we do?

We breathe the same air
But then it looks like no one cares
They just see us signing on
And our self respect is gone

You and I
We live our lives and then we die
In between
We care about the one we've been
And we too
Want to work and earn our dues
But who cares
When there isn't any work
Today
Tomorrow
We're sorry but it's true
And there's nothing we can do

Look into my eyes
And see the soul behind my smile
It's honest and it's true
I'm a person just like you.

SONG END:

<u>SCENE FIFTEEN:</u>

STREET SCENE:

WOMAN
They've launched the last sub at Lairds.

WOMAN
The Unicorn.

WOMAN
HMS Unicorn if you don't mind!

WOMAN
Our country will always be safe with what they've built down the yard.

WOMAN
But no more.

WOMAN
It won't be long before it's opened again.

WOMAN
They'll be building more.

WOMAN
There'll be more work soon.

WOMAN
It never stays quiet for long.

WOMAN
Ship building in this country won't survive without our lads down the yard.

TWO MANAGERS:

MAN
Another good job.

MAN
The quietest submarines around.

MAN
Amazing vessels.

MAN
Built by the men.

MAN
We should continue to be proud of the work done at Lairds.

MAN
Doesn't seem right to let the men know they won't be using them.

MAN
No…surplus to requirements

MAN
The Ministry doesn't want them.

MAN
It's up to them – they paid for the three of them.

MAN
No the taxpayers paid for the three of them. It all came from the taxpayer's pocket.

MAN
What a waste.

MAN
They'll be sold off to the highest bidder.

MAN
At a fraction of the price.

MAN
If at all.

WORKFORCE:

MAN
Where's all the work that was promised?

MAN
Just not coming our way.

MAN
Vickers is getting it all.

MAN
Vickers is in charge.

MAN
But what about Lairds? What about other work.

MAN
Seems no one wants to give to us.

MAN
I heard someone say – if it floats they won't let it get built at Lairds.

MAN
It not right – something's not right about it.

MAN
Others are making decisions about the destiny of the yard.

MAN
Someone doesn't want us to work.

MAN
They want Lairds shut down.

MAN
They don't care about Lairds anymore.

MAN
Looks like the end.

SCENE SIXTEEN:

BUSY STREET:

WOMAN
We'll get by love.

WOMAN
We always do.

WOMAN
It's Birkenhead for ye'

WOMAN
Who's for tea?

MAN
Are you going to Tranmere tonight?

MAN
Wouldn't miss it. I never do.

MAN
I'll see you there – same spot.

MAN
Yeah alright. It's going to be a hard game tonight so don't build your hopes up.

MAN
Its Tranmere...I never do, but I always go.

WOMAN
Seen you in town today love – buy much.

WOMAN
You know I never do but I still go into town every other day and look at the same shops.

WOMAN
Same here.

WOMAN
I just like town.

WOMAN
Everybody does!

KID
Mum Can I go the Warners with me pocket money?

KID
I'll see you at the Europa in an hour.

KID
Are you coming the park for a game of footy – there's going to be a gang of us.

KID
Mum! Our Mario's been banned from the trams at Woodside – they caught him peeing out the window again.

WOMAN
Mario! Get in here now you little sod.

MAN
See you down the Cross tonight.

MAN
Yeah, we'll all be there.

MAN
Karaoke at Yates.

MAN
I better go early then to make sure I've had enough to sing.

WOMAN
Mario! If you don't get here now I'll kill you.

WOMAN
Nice day today.

WOMAN
Its lovely isn't it.

WOMAN
I'm sitting on my step.

WOMAN
I might join ye'.

WOMAN
Me too. Hey Barbara, Get your decky out we're sitting on the steps.

WOMAN
Great! I've got a cold bottle of wine in the fridge.

WOMAN
Me too!

MAN
I'll see you later love, I'm on a late shift.

WOMAN
Tarra Love.

MAN
Back to work.

MUSIC TO DOWN OUR STREET STARTS AS:

WILLIAM LAIRD
I believe Birkenhead is the place to be. I believe Birkenhead should, and will, be the centre of our countries industrial growth, the place where man shall dwell with man whatever their income or status, whatever the situation the Lord has granted them.

A & P
The A&P group purchased the ship yard in August 2001…..concentrating on the ship repair market.

WOMAN
Many people have stories, opinions and moans but most have their pride and many laughs.

WILLIAM LAIRD
I believe Birkenhead to be the new town of this country with good housing through efficient and innovative planning, adequate hygiene, a local hospital public libraries, public parks and facilities for the good people of this town that shall be the envy of the country.

MAN
We know what's happened over the last few years. It's been a disappointment and, in many ways a injustice, but the people are still here, the town's still alive. People seem happy with their lot.

A & P
The combination of A & P's well established project management experience together with the high levels of local marine engineering skills has received an enthusiastic response from ship owners and the yard now looks forward to a bright future.

WILLIAM LAIRD
People will flock from miles around to see how a town should work and how under the shadow of the greatest ship builders in this country, a town can grow and prosper.

WOMAN
We should be proud of our heritage.

MAN
....Proud of the people of this town from its early beginnings to this moment now.

WOMAN
We should look at the positives, look around and see the people who continue to work in, around and for this town.

WILLIAM LAIRD
I William Laird will see this through and with the opening of the new shipyard at the Birkenhead pool, Lairds will be nearer for the workers as well as providing more work for the local people and people who choose to come and live in this wonderful place.

FRANK FIELD
Any history of Cammell Laird is a history of Birkenhead…And here is our history….

WOMAN
We should be proud of our people

MAN
We should be proud of Cammell Lairds.

MAN
We should be proud of Birkenhead

WOMAN
It all happened and will continue to happen…

ALL
…down our street.

SINGING STARTS UNDER LAIRDS SPEECH:

Down our street
Where the people that you meet seem really happy
Down our street

Down our street
Where the people there will greet you with a smile or two
Down our street

Our doors are always open
The Kettle's always on
You're welcome for a cuppa
Where ever you are from
Don't hesitate to ask us
To lend a helping hand
We're working hard to make this the best town in the land

Down our street
Where everyone knows everyone to look out for
Down our street

Down our street
You'll hear the sound of chatter and of laughter
Down our street

There's people there to help you
Or to have a good old moan
That's what makes the bricks and mortar
Into a homes
And when you need a bob or two
Or a bed just for the night
The people here will help you
These People are alright

Down our street
Where the people that you meet seem really happy
Down our street

Down our street
Where the people there will greet you with a smile or two
Down our street

The cold long nights of winter when the fire's always alight
Doesn't dampen the spirits in the long winter nights
Doesn't fade the feeling that this is where you're from
Everybody knows you for here's where you belong

Down our street
Where the people that you meet seem really happy
Down our street

Down our street
Where the people there will greet you with a smile or two
This is just for you
Down our street.

END